PINKY PROMISE

Gina Sollow

Contents

Her dad is dead, brother is just like any sibling, mom and kids at school don't like her. She fell in love with her best friend and he fell in love with her. Everything seems to be getting better. But when Mitchell might have to move to the other side of the country she isn't sure what will happen.

Chapter 1

Chapter 1

S he made her way through the obnoxious students talking, laughing, yelling. It was all a blur to her though, she didn't care if anyone was talking to her, laughing about her, or yelling at her. she was just determined to go to class. Not because she just loves math, but because him. He can literally turn her frown upside down. And any other way he feels. He isn't like the others who judge her. He accepts her for who she is.

Oh ya she is, well, me. Allow me to introduce myself 14-year-old Regina simon. Reg or rae or regi for short or anything else. For some reason I am not liked in school everyone hates me and spreads rumors. Mitch always says to ignore them. I try but everyday they think of something I hate even more. Mitchell is a 15 year old that is a totally hotty!!! And he is lucky enough to call me best-friend. And I am even luckier to be able to say it back. Everyday mat thinks of something to make me smile. But if he doesn't something serious is probably going on. But I wouldn't know cause that's never happened.

I finally got to math and there he was sitting in my seat (insert sigh with blush.) He thought his seat (even though it was right next to mine) wasn't close enough to me. So everyday I would find him in my seat. Then I would shove him off onto the floor, and start laughing while he faked some pain. "Rae!! That hurt I think I broke something!" Mitch whispered in 'pain'. "oh shut up Mitch quit being a wimp!"

"DIIIINNNGGG!!!!!!" hallelujah school was over. As I hurried to the bus I could already see Mitch in our usual seats waiting. He waved. Now I could now see the grass even better thanks to being tripped. When I looked back up at Mitch his face was a mess. He must've seen that. He is very protective with me especially when I'm tripped. I don't know why, I don't think he likes seeing scrapes and cuts on me. Thank goodness he hasn't payed any attention to my wrists lately.

Once I sat down he said "you ok?" "ya, I'm fine." "they are gonna get it tomorrow!" " Mitch please don't! Not again! Remember last time you beat someone up for me I just got picked on more because 'I was a cry baby and needed someone to take care of me'?" "ya, but, I don't like you being hurt. I've been trying to contain myself with all the name calling you get but it tears me apart! Ya know, someday I'm just going to punch 'em all right-" " Mitch." "fiiiinnee"

The bus came to an abrupt stop mat and I got off. Mitch insisted I was hurt and he give me a piggy-back-ride down the dirt road. I had no choice. We finally got home. (We were neighbors.) "Remeber no more beating them up right?" "Right!" he responded. "Pinky promise?" I asked. We both locked our pinkies together and kissed our (own) hands where our thumbs were. He responded with "pink promise!"

Chapter 2

"He used his left hand!" I though as I woke up spontaneously. Mitch and I always pinky promised with our right hands. The only way we agreed it could be broken was if we used our left hand or didn't make eye-contact without the other person noticing.

My brother took me to school in the mornings but he was 'too busy' with his girlfriend after school to take me home, so the bus it was. So after he dropped me off started down the hall to math. Ugh here comes the names, looks, and laughs. I try to get through it all.

Mitch isn't in my seat! I knew it! I knew he would punch them again. As I took my seat Mr.Leo started taking attendance once. "Mitchell Jackson?"

There was a loud response of "detention" "oh" was all Mr.Leo said.

The most annoying kid in school yelled in a mocking voice "did you need someone to be your daddy since he is actually dead?"

I had it! "SHUT UP!!" I yelled and smacked him across the face.

"Ms.Simon! Detention, NOW!" Again the room responded with "ooooooooohhhh"

Mat gave me a terribly confused look as I sneaked into detention. I mouthed to him 'why?' he just looked down. Detention was terrible. I wasn't even allowed to look up.

Mitch and I didn't speak at all on the bus for a while. Finally I spoke "why did you do that?" "Rae I had to!"

"No you didn't I told you-" he cut me off.

"I don't care what you told me Regi! I was sick of it!" "I'm sick o-" "Oh! my! goodness! And I didn't see you doing anything about it! I care about you! I love you! You don't even realize how much I love you! My job is to protect you! Your dad told me to! He knew he wasn't going to be around but I was. So I had to do something! Now you need to know that I will go to detention as much as I need as long as I am protecting you!"

I started balling like a baby. I fell into his arms as he wrapped them around me tightly. All of these thoughts filled my mind. Mitchell loved me?! Dad knew he wouldn't be around? Mitch cared soo much? MITCH LOVED ME!???

I've loved Mitch forever but to know he loves me back, brings tears of joy. But tears of sadness because I never knew how much he cared. So I guess you could say I cried myself to sleep that night.

Chapter 3

I woke up to my phone going off like an overdramatic girl who's boyfriend just broke up with her after 2 hours.

They were all from Mitch. Omg. Could he just let me sleep, it's Saturday. I read the texts.

'rae get up.' 'Regi.' 'chicka are you busy today?' 'regina' 'wanna go to the movies?' 'why did you cry yesterday?' 'regina'. And they kept coming.

I wanted to throw the phone. But I just responded with 'I was busy sleeping. What movie? And I was being over-dramatic.'

He texted back within like 3 seconds. "oh sorry. "The boy in the striped pajamas" it came out yesterday. I thought we could go with Drew and Amanda." they were pretty much our only other friends from school.

My cell phone rang it was Mitchell. "hello." "hey I thought this might be an easier way to talk to you. So are you cool with the movies with Drew and Amanda?"

"ya sounds great I just gotta actually look presentable for the day."

"ok and this isnt like a double date or anything unless you want it to be but that might be awkward so it's fine with me if you don't wanna go or not but-"

I cut him off, he was too shy to actually straight up ask me on a date so I made it easy for him. "Double date sounds good!"

" oh. Umm.. Well.. Uhh..ya sounds wonderful oh the movie starts at 9 so you've got lots of time to get ready."

"okay well I'll talk to you later my brothers yelling at me bye"

"bye"

IM GOING ON A DATE WITH MITCHELL JACK-SOOOOONNNNNNNN!!!!!!!!!!!!!!!!!!!!!!!!!!!!¡¡!!!!!!! AHHHH-HHHHH

I ran downstairs yelling it at my brother "JASONJASONJASON-JASON!!!!! IM GOING ON A DATE WITH MITCH!!!!!"

" the one creeper kid next door?"

" no the on sweet hot kid next door"

"oh him! Does he know the rules of dating my sister? Cuz he better learn them!"

"oh Jason it's only one date! He didn't even necessarily call it a date, but he implied it."

"so he still has boundaries. And he will learn them tonight!"

"whatever" I said sarcastically while walking away to get ready.

sorry its short I couldnt think about what to add. let me know what you think about it so far please!

Chapter 4

Chapter 4

WARNING IF YOU HAVE NEVER SEEM THE MOVIE 'THE BOY IN THE STRIPED PAJAMAS' I AM ABOUT TO SOME-WHAT SPOIL IT IN THIS CHAPTER. SO IF YOU DON'T WANT ONE OF THE SADDEST MOVIES EVER RUINED FOR YOU, GO WATCH IT BEFORE YOU READ THIS!

The doorbell rang at 7:15 on the dot. Since we live out in the country more it's takes us longer to get into town. Jason opened the door and started his lecture about 'dating rules'

"now, no starring at her with googly eyes. No holding hands, no hugging, no kissing, none of that, so pretty much no touching her. The 'I have to stretch' move is off limits. Give her your sweatshirt is too. Don't sit so close to her."

He had lots more to say but I got tired of it "Jason shut up we have leave now" I said as sweetly as possible.

Once we got in the vehicle Mitch started it up and we were on our way. Mat turned on the radio.

"oh no that was my favorite song and it's over!" I said as he went to a station.

"what song was it?"

"all of me by John Legend"

"never heard it"

"it's such a beautiful song"

"so was your brother really serious about the rules?"

"hahaha he might've been but oh well."

"so they weren't from your mom?"

"no my mom wouldn't even have any rules she probably would've just said be back in 3 days max"

"oh"

"No I can pay for it!"

"nope if this is a date I'm paying for it!"

I just glared at him.

"theater 3" the cashier said with a smirk on his face

"thank you" I replied.

"Mitch you don't need to get me any popcorn either!"

"fine a drink?"

"no!!!!!"

"fine looks your getting candy. What kind? Wait! I already know. One box of sweet tarts please" Good choice. My favorite.

"here you go" the familiar friend running concessions said.

We walked into the movie room, met up with drew and amanda and took our seats.

The lights went down. As the movie started I quickly found out that "The Boy In The Striped Pajamas" was about the holocaust. Oh. Boy. I can tell I will probably end up crying.

The first 'rule' Mat broke was the 'I have to stretch'. As he started moving his arm down, reached up my hand and pulled it down around my shoulder and leaned on his shoulder. 1st rule broken.

This movie had me having chills the whole entire time! Dude this is so depressing. Next thing I knew i had Mitch's sweatshirt on. What?! I had no choice!

2nd rule broken.

And in the movie I found this innocent, uneducated about what was going on, 7-year-old, digging under the electric fence to help a boy in the camp find his dad.

And the tears started. Nonononononononoonononononoooooo why were they talking them into a dark room. Oh nonononono. No no they're gonna gas the people in the camps! No. I can't do this! Mitch could tell I didn't like this and pulled me closer. OH MY GOODNESS NOT THE TWO BOYS TOO!!!! AHHHHH!!!! NOOOO!!! OH MY GOODNESS DID THEY JUST GAS TO DEATH TWO INNOCENT LITTLE BOYS!!!! THEY DIED HOLDING HANDS TOO!!!!!

I was balling at this point. And so was Mat, Drew, and Amanda. I found my hand interlocked with Mitch's. I looked at him with a tear rolling down my face. He wiped it away and leaned in.

Chapter 5

Chapter 5

I felt his lips brush past my lips and past my cheek to my ear. I felt butterflies in my stomach, and my heart get beat up a little. He whispered in my ear.

"I'm sorry I didn't know it was gonna be so sad. Will you be okay tonight?"

He knew even the mention of the holocaust upset me. "I think so if not I'll wake you up with calls and texts until you come over."

"ok"

Our hands were still interlocked. He turned to the left to say bye to Drew as I turned to Amanda.

"Holding hands now?!?!" She asked like a girly girl.

"I was just...scared during the movie."

"I'm sure that's what it was. Wink. Wink."

I heard Mitch and Drew whisper behind me: "dude did you kiss her yet?!"

"Drew! I don't think I'm gonna kiss her on the first date!"

"You were so close! See what you gotta do-" their voices got quieter.

I gave the concession stand guy a friendly smile and wave as we left.

"Who's that?" Mitch asked

"One of Jason's friends."

"Isn't he in our grade?."

"He is. Jason has a lot of friends in different grades in high school."

"oh"

Inside of me I think my heart was kicked or punched with every word he spoke. WHY DID WE HAVE TO ALMOST KISS?!!!!!!!! I felt a tear starting to form everything went black and white and Mitch was rushing toward me.

Next thing I knew my face was being poked, and I was in Mitchs driveway, in Mitch's truck.

"What happened?"

"you pasted out and I had to carry you to the truck."

"oh I see"

"well I'll walk you to your house....next door....haha."

"ok haha"

He seemed to be walking very slowly like he didn't want to take me home. We reached my front porch and he sat on the swing. I sat next to him with my head on his shoulder.

"Truth or dare?"

"Mitch?" I asked with a voice sounding like I was saying 'really?'

"No, I'm serious!"

"ok, truth."

"would you rather have had lived during the holocaust with me or now without me?"

Oh my goodness could there be a harder question? I turned and slid down so I was laying on my back, head on Mitchs lap, his fingers playing with my hair, and feet hanging of the side of the swing.

"well if I choose now without you I wouldn't have had this question. But if I choose then without you and I died that would be payback for asking this question. So then, with you"

I made no sense. I started to fall asleep on the swing.

"Maybe you should go in now?"

"Ya probably. I had a great time tonight! Maybe we could do it again sometime?"

"ya sounds cool!"

We were standing face to face in front of the door like in the movies. He looked me in the eyes then at my lips and back to my eyes.

"Do you know you're beautiful?" he asked.

He started leaning closer to me. ARE WE ACTUALLY GONNA KISS!?!?!!!!!!!!!!!!!! Just then the stupid door opened. Stupid Jason.

"Mitchell don't you need to get home?" Jason asked.

He nodded. He waved goodbye and I went inside.

"JASON I'M GONNA PUNCH YOU FOR THAT!!!!!"

"HAHAHAHHAHAHAHAHAHHAHAHAHAHHAHAHA-HAHAHHAHAHAHAHHAHAHAHHAHAHAHAHHA-HAHAHAHAHH well you already got to the maximum of rules you can break everyday. Which is 4 btw."

I just gave him a glare as I went up to my room.

Chapter 6

Chapter 6

I was being taken away. Kicking and screaming as much as I could. Scrapes an bruises all over me. No one heard me. No one cared. I found myself yelling for Mitch. He didn't come and help me. Dragged down the stairs around corners. Taken out the door, I tried to hold on to the frame. I was in a strange car going to the middle of no where. No chance of being heard now. I felt ropes around my hands and feet, gag in my mouth, blade against me neck, and gun to my head. I had gone numb to everything and couldn't move. My world stopped. Kneeling on the ground. I heard a noise from the gun. All they had to do now was pull the trigger and I would be gone. Where was Jason why didn't he save me when I yelled? I heard the hands slowly move to the trigger. And I heard one last click.

"MITCH!!" I screamed as I woke up shaking, in tears. I just sat there, for 1 minuet and 23 seconds. Then Mitch was by my side comforting me.

"shhhh. It's ok. I'm here." he said with his arms around me.

"Mitch t-they took me a-away. And I screamed b-but no one came and they t-tied me up and there was a k-knife and a g-gun" I stuttered through my tears.

"It's ok it was just a nightmare. It's all over. It won't happen. You're okay. I'm here" he kissed my forehead. "Its ok, wait here"

He was back within 4 minuets. With French toast with syrup, strawberries, and apple juice.

"Did my mom cook this morning?"

"yep. Why didn't she come up when you screamed? I mean I'd much rather be here with you than ya know sleeping quietly at home."

"She either didn't hear, thought you were here and I was just yelling at you, or best guess didn't care."

"That was the loudest yell ever if I heard it in my room. I'm really sorry about all of that with your mom. It seems hard."

"Kind of, but it's been like this forever. And don't be sorry, it just builds me up some, and makes me even more grateful for you."

"ok if you say so. Hey meet me in the woods by the river at 12:20 k?"

"um ok but why?"

"just because" he left

I finished my breakfast, took the dishes down stairs, and came back to my room without saying anything to my mom. Put on a pair of shorts, a white cami and a loose tank-top, with a blue ombré design. I had the cami because otherwise Jason would yell at me. He was like my mom that I didn't have. I put my hair into a donut bun, with my side-swept bangs down, hairsprayed it and called it good.

Oh shoot! 12:15! Five minuets. The woods was me and Mitchs favorite place. It was right behind our houses. We had a fort built in a group of weeping willow trees, they were my favorite. We would always go there when we just needed a break from life. That's where I spent most of my time.

I saw Mitch sitting on the big rock by the river. He looked so...sooo.....chill? So I didn't think anything was wrong. I snuck up behind him wrapping my arms around his shoulders and neck.

"hey! You're late!" he kissed my cheek.

"well I'm sorry I need clothes."

"oh"

"So why did you drag me out here?"

"Oh actually there is no reason. I just wanted to be with you. Not with your mom too."

"Oh I see."

He stood up while I stood on the rock. He picked me up like they sometimes do at weddings.

"and, I wanted to THROW YOU INTO THE RIVER!!"

" N O N O N O N O N O N O N O N O N O N O M I T C H NOOOOOO!!!" I screamed as he was running down the dock.

He stopes and set me down right on the edge where I almost fell in. As I was loosing my balance he wrapped his arms around me pulling me close so I didn't fall. We made eye contact. He glanced at my lips. I wanted to kiss him so bad! But making it so he fell into the water sounded much better. I mean why should he get rewarded for almost making me drown? So I quickly turned and threw him in. And to my luck he was still holding on to me and soon I was under too.

We were both above when I started talking. "MATHEW JACK-SON!!!! IM GOING TO-"

But I was cut of by Mitch silencing me. "will this make up for it?"

He leaned in and kissed me.

Chapter 7

Chapter 7

"Ok students pick up your things and go to the walls. We are getting a new seating chart. Yay!"

There were murmurs of disappointment. Oh no this means I won't be next to Mitch anymore! Ugh I'm going to die if I get put next to a jerk.

"Thomas here, Regina here, then christopher."

Ugh Thomas. He's the one I slapped.

"hey, I'm really truly sorry about everything I've said about you and especially the other day about your dad." Thomas sounded really sweet

"I really appreciated that. Thank you!"

"oh and happy to hear about you and Mitch."

"haha thanks." I said while blushing.

Maybe he wasn't so bad. I wonder what made him change so much over the weekend.

"ok remember we have an exam next week. Don't forget to study and get help of you need. Have a good day."

I went to my locker and Mitch was standing in front of it. I could still feel his lips on mine from last night at the river.

"what your locker combo?"

"why?"

"because I want to open your locker."

"17-3-10"

"dude! Why is it so clean?!"

"I can't live with messy"

"your room?"

"that's a different story."

"come on! Hurry up! You're so slow!!"

"well sorry I pretty much carry around dead bodies"

"hope that's never me in there!"

"who knows, you better watch your back!"

"I don't have eyes in the back of my head though!"

"well, get some."

"hey I'll just meet you on the bus I have to talk to someone after school."

"who?"

"uhh....someone...."

"you're not cheating on me are you?!"

"NO MITCH!! Have you looked at the other guys in this school?! You are the only cute one!"

"awww you think I'm cute?"

"No I think you're a total hotty."

Did I just say that? Oops to late

"ya, I get that a lot." he flipped his hair. Mmmmmm why did he do that he looks so adorable when he does that!

"will you just go to science already ?"

"see ya later hot stuff"

"don't call me that"

He turned and winked. Oh how I hated how sweet he was.

I went into art. Everyone told me how good of a singer I was and how pretty I was and a great artist (not to be stuck up or vain or anything though). But I didn't see the big deal lots of people have talents. Mitch always says how I should draw him but I don't want to. So today I finished my project early, so I started drawing for Mitch. I drew him and me, jumping off the dock at the river. Why? Because it reminds me of the day he kissed me. I hope he thinks of that too, I hope it makes him realize that I liked that day.

The bell rang and I pretty much ran to Mitch's locker. That was the 'someone' I had to talk to. I slid the drawing through one of the slits in the locker door. nobody questioned me so that was good.

Why did Mitch choose the back of the bus? Those seats are like a couch. So more people sat there. I went back there and sat down.

"hey hot stuff!" I winked at Mitch

"hey beautiful!" and wrapped his arm around me. I took his other arm and felt it. Man did he have muscles!

"strong enough?"

"I don't know never had to check"

"what?"

"I'll know once I use my muscle to save you."

I started leaning off the seat to see if Mitch would catch me. He let me fall.

"Oops I guess I'm not"

"ow"

"you need me to kiss it better?"

"yes."

"where?"

"right here" I said pointing to a random spot on my arm. He slightly punched my mouth.

"how about there?"

"hhhmmmm don't think so hehe"

He now slightly punched again but with sound effects.

"now?"

I just smiled

"would you like a kiss?"

"well it's not exactly a kiss its just-"

"just say yes you idiot!"

"yes"

"too bad!" and I stuck my tongue out at him like a little kid.

Chapter 8

Tuesday. Oh wonderful. Mondays were bad enough but Tuesday's. Actually they were fine I just didn't like the thought of mornings. But this week wasn't too bad. We had thursday and Friday off and Wensday was the last school dance of the year. So I only had tonight of boring homework and the rest of the days probably with Mitch.

I go ready like usual. Changed my clothes. Did my hair. Went downstairs to eat. Jason wasn't up like usual though. My mom walked in.

"Jason is sick so I'm going to take you."

"ok"

"and Ava is going to pick you up after school"

"oh ya"

And that was the start and end to our conversation. If we ever talked more than that if would just be he asking if I needed or wanted anything from the store. And it was mostly my part for talking anyway.

Ava was Jason's girl friend she was taking me shooing for a dress for the dance. If I ever wanted to go shopping she was the girl to call. I have so much fun with her and we get the cutest things.

"come on! hurry up! Lets go!"

"I'm coming! hold on! Just a minuet!"

"I don't have just a minuet! I have to be at work! Im already taking off time to get you to school." my mom sounded very rude.

"Well then why didn't I just get a ride with Mitch?"

"that boy across the path?! Absolutely not! Why do you think you can take advantage if that sweet dear family?! Ya know why couldn't you be like them?! Why can't you be perfect, pretty, skinny, and better than what you are now? Why do you have to be such a stuck up little vain jerk!! Do you realize how much time and money I spend on you?! You child, are impossible! and terrible! And so worthless. There are more words that could be used to describe you but I'd rather not say them!" my mom yelled. I wish I had sat in the back so she wouldn't see my eyes start to fill up with tears.

"Why are you crying?! You know it's all true! You making me feel bad isn't going to work you little-- nevermind I won't say that word"

We were at the school and she didn't stop the car all the way when I got out. I stepped out and started balling trying not to be noticed by people. I just wanted to be with Mitch in his arms. With him making me feel better.

"hey what's up?" I was stopped in my walking by Thomas.

"doesn't Matter"

"you're balling like a baby I think it matters"

"have you seen Mitch?"

"not going to tell you if he is at our locker until you tell me."

"move"

I pushed him out of the way. I didn't even get to look at Mitch's face. All I knew was he had his arms around me an his shirt was about to be soaked.

"What happened? Do I need to punch someone?"

"I talked to my mom."

"that's good?"

"actually she talked to me. She said 'why can't you be perfect, pretty, skinny, and better than you are now.' she said I was impossible, terrible, stuck up, vain, and worthless."

"no no no! Get those words out if your mind. You're perfect the way you are! You're beautiful and gorgeous! I don't want anything about you to change! You're wonderful an priceless!! And I better not see those scars on your wrists anymore!" he frowned

His shirt was completely covered in my tears.

"thank you Mitch"

"anytime precious, so we clear about that?"

"yes sir"

"good. Oh and I got your note. I liked it but was it supposed to mean something?"

"the other day. When you shut me up with a kiss."

"oh, ya." he blushed and did that cute little thing when he scratches his neck then leaves it there like he is deep in thought.

"yeah, that was a good day"

"wonderful day. Hey guess what tomorrow is!!!!"

"the dance"

"aaaannnddd"

"wensday?"

"YOUR BIRTHDAY!!!"

"that doesn't really Matter."

"yes it does!!"

"mmhhmmm no"

"what do you want?"

"nothing"

"what do you want?!"

"my mom to not hate me. My dad to be alive. People not to bully me. Me to not be so me. And just my life to have love"

"anything that I could actually get you?"

"your presence tomorrow."

"fine I'll just think of something."

"you have fun with that!"

"I will"

"Make sure it's not something like socks"

"anything for you."

Chapter 9

"This one is kinda cute"

"like my face! But my face is cuter."

"Ava you have problems"

"i know! Go try those on I'll keep looking."

"fine"

Ew that makes me look fat.

Too short

Too long

Too big

Too small

Too pink

Too sparkly

Too boring

Too just no

"anything working?"

"absolutely not!"

"try this"

"that's ugly!"

"haha I know! This one then!"

It was a grey ombré high-low flowy type dress. She new me too well. Ombré and high-low flowy type dresses were da bomb! I put it on and it was perfect. I opened up my fitting room door to see Ava standing there. So the only thing in my nature was to start posing

"ok just stop now. Like it?"

"haha ya it's great!"

"sweet let's go you're brother just texted me to hurry up"

"he can wait"

"oh no it wasn't for me. That friendly boy across your road is chilling at your house waiting for you."

"that would be Mitch"

"what did you get? Go put it on so I can see it!"

"no Mitch you are going to have to wait!"

"but!"

"why are you lookin at my butt?"

"I wasn't! I said it with it being Spelt with only one t"

"uhhhuh."

"it's true."

"I want to go to sleep!"

"then go to sleep"

"I can't your here."

"then I'll leave"

"no I don't want you to leave"

"but what about you sleeping?"

"I can wait"

"movie?"

"sure."

"what one?"

"you pick. I'm too lazy to get up."

"Alice in wonderland?"

"I don't care."

"ok that's a no. Ummm. You have too many movies to choose from. Dolphin tale? You like that right?"

"no find a live story!"

"ugh. Beauty and the beast?"

"sure." he put the movie in and I curled up next to him on the couch with his arm around me.

I was trying my best not to fall asleep. But Mitch wasn't helping with that. He gave me his sweatshirt (and boy did it smell good!) then he made a nice spot perfect for me to fall asleep. He probably had it all planned out: the movie, the pillows and blankets. All to make me sleep. That sweet, loving jerk!

I won't fall asleep.

I won't fall asleep.

I won't fall asleep.

All I remember from the movie is something about being a guest. I don't know it was beauty and the beast. I did fall asleep.

And when I woke up I was in Mitch's arms. He was taking me to my room because it was late. How long was it since the movie was over? Was he just watching me sleep? Anyway. I didn't want him to think he woke me up so closed my eyes again and tried not to move. He put me in my bed, pulled the coverers up to my shoulders, (did I still have on his sweatshirt?) and kissed my forehead. That weirdo. I took my hands out from under the blankets and pulled his head toward mine just before he turned to leave. His lips met the corner of mine.

"goodnight Mitch."

"night gorgeous!"

Chapter 10

Chapter 10

June 4th. I got home from school with flowers and a balloon sitting in my room next to Ava just sitting on my bed. Mitch got me flowers and a balloon too, also chocolates, a big stuffed bear, movies.

"ok hurry up. I don't have all day to do your hair."

I threw my stuff down put on a button up shirt, so latter when I took it off, to put on the dress, it wouldn't ruin my hair, and sat in front of the mirror while Ava started curling my hair.

"can you get my phone off the bed?"

"hold this" handing me the curling iron. "what's this" she said in a girly voice.

I rolled my eyes.

"Mitch's sweatshirt, he forgot it last night."

"really?"

"and possibly the other one in the top drawer....."

She just laughed.

"what don't you have one of Jason's sweatshirts?"

"ok maybe but doesn't Matter"

"my phone"

"oh ya. Your boyfriend says he loves you and can't wait to see you tonight and"

"give me my phone. No he didn't. All he said was what time, you jerk"

"no read the messages before that"

"oh"

"ya, you jerk"

"dude hurry up it's 4 already!"

"so?"

"Mitch will be here at 6"

"oh! Well I'm done with your hair. Makeup now"

"well hurry up please"

"do you want more pink or red colors"

"pink. Red is to 'hey look at me'"

"ok. Don't you want your boyfriend to notice you though?"

"considering he is my boyfriend I think he will notice me. And Mitch doesn't like me wearing makeup that much anyway."

"oh"

For the next while I was told to close my eyes, pucker my lips, smile, and all sorts of other thing while Ava did my makeup.

"ok go change then I will add jewelry."

I took off my button up shirt and jeggings trading them for the dress. I fell quite a few times in the process of getting the dress on. I went back to my room and was bombarded with Ava putting a necklace, bracelet, and ear rings on me.

"Ok let's quickly go get some food before Mitch gets here"

We went down stairs and turned to see Mitch sitting on the couch. Ava dragged me Back around the corner and up the stairs to my room.

"ill get food you stay here"

"fine"

I heard Mitch ask if he could come up and see me. But Ava wasn't going to let that happen. While I waited I found some shoes and other things I needed. Poked a hole into on of the balloons to get the helium.

In a high pitched helium voice "hi Ava"

She busted up laughing

"did you know it's hard reasoning with Mitch?"

"ok it's 6:01"

"ok"

I went down the stairs turned and saw Mitch still sitting in the couch. He turned his head and stood up.

MITCHELL'S P.O.V

She was beautiful. I wanted to start dancing with her right there. She was gorgeous. Simply gorgeous.

"wow! You look amazing!"

"thanks" she blushed and put her bangs behind her ear.

"we should probably get going. If it starts at 6:30"

"ya. Bye Ava thanks for everything!"

In the truck I held her hand. It was so soft and delicate like a baby bird. It was too quiet. I figured this would be a good time to talk to her.

"hey I have to tell you something."

Chapter 11

Chapter 11

H is voice sounded sad.

"first do you know I think you're really beautiful."

I didn't know what to say.

"umm. So. In a couple of days my family and I will be going on 'vacation' but it's also to try to find a good spot to live because my dad night have to move for work."

"move?"

"ya"

"where?"

"Washington"

"no! That's too far from Florida! Too far from me! No no no. I can't loose you too!"

"it's not necessarily set in stone that we are moving but it's close."

"no I won't let you. Why can't you just stay. And live with your grandma or something?"

"because I don't want to go to knitting on Monday, bingo on Tuesday, or anything else the other days every day."

"then your aunt?"

"she moved"

"no just no"

"how about we just enjoy ourselves tonight and think about this some other time. Besides it's your birthday too."

"ya and all you got me was chocolate."

"I got you more then that! Also I'm letting you keep that sweatshirt from last night"

"what about the one from the movies?"

"what?! You have two of them? Fine keep them both"

"I was going to keep them anyway"

"oh alrighty"

We found an empty spot in the parking lot near the back. All the rest were taken.

"don't get out yet"

"umm ok...."

He got out came around to my side of the truck opened the door and put his hand out for me. I took it and got out of the truck. He wrapped his arm around my waist and we started inside.

The room was filled with people. Most people were dancing to the music, others were either; twerking, making out, or eating food. I wasn't a pretty site. Slow dancing in a burning room by John Mayer started playing and Mitch started talking to drew.

"Mitch we have to dance!"

"hold on"

"no I cant one of my songs is on!"

He wouldn't budge. I dragged him out to the dance floor. He just stood there straight faced. I did my puppy dog face. He put out his bottom lip. I just shook my head no. He finally gave in and put his hands around my waist with my arms around his neck and my head on his shoulder. I noticed he kept looking around the room.

"what are you looking for?"

"Making sure the room isn't burning."

"oh my goodness....."

Brenda and her little 'click' were walking toward me and Mitch when we were standing off to the side.

"hey Regina can I talk to you over here for a minute?" of the girls asked.

"uh sure."

I saw Brenda gettin all up in Mitch's business.

"so Mitch. The next song. You wanna dance with me?"

"uh no thanks."

"but Mitch" get your hands off my boy! "I requested it just for you and me"

I started to turn but I was stopped by the girl who wanted to talk to me, pulling me around.

"Regina umm... Where did you get your dress?"

I dont know what I said or what the rest of the conversation was. I was listening to Brenda and Mitch.

"come let's go dance!"

"no"

"no?! Oh nonono you do not say no to me. Now let's go."

She dragged him into the crowd. It was to large to even begin to look for him. Thomas as the whole thing and came and sat and talked with me while I waited for Mitch to return. He came back 20 minutes later hair messed up, shirt untucked, tie undone, and out of breath from running away.

"Mitch wait! Come back!" Brenda yelled from being stuck in the crowd. I saw Thomas go up and say something to her. Who knows what but it made her smile and blush. She took his and and led him somewhere. He turned behind him and mouthed with an evil look 'you're welcome.'

"worst 20 minutes of my life! There was no escape! She wouldn't back off!"

"let me fix your tie and hair but you fix your shirt first."

He mirrored me fixing his tie like I had a tie on. Then the same with his hair. Running my fingers through his hair to fix it and he not touching my hair because he knew he would mess up the curls.

"I'll be right back I'm going to go talk to drew for a bit since you dragged me away earlier."

"haha ok"

A teacher came up and asked me: "are you Regina Simon?"

"yes"

"this is for you" she handed me a not and walked away.

I read it and tears started to fill my eyes. Not dad all over! no don't let it be dad all over!

"Mitchell we have to go"

"huh?"

"we have to go!"

I shoved the note into his chest. He read it.

"sorry gotta go drew!"

We started running to Mitchs truck.

"hey listen to me" Mitch started in the truck. "he's going to be fine. This won't be your dad again. Understand? He will be fine."

The words I read kept repeating in my mind.

'Jason's Car collided with a semi into a tree -Ava'

~~~~~~~~~~~~~~~~~~~~~~

Hey let me know what you think so far! An also if you haven't read the description I added go do that. The last part let's you know a bit about parts of the story. But it you don't care fine with me. Hope you enjoy this and I'm trying to update as much as possible.

Chapter 12

Chapter 12

"Where's Jason at?"

"he went into get x-rays. I haven't seen him yet. The semi driver called 911 actually. Jason passed out so they didn't get to ask him anything."

I was pacing within two steps. Mitch and Ava tried to calm me down but it didn't work. I kept mumbling "not dad again. Not dad again."

"Rae this will not be your dad again!"

"you never know. Is my mom here?"

"no, I called her but she said she couldn't come right now because she was busy."

I just rolled my eyes. I wish dad were here. Dad would've been the first one here. He would've been the first one even if we just fell off the scooter.

"Are you guys waiting for Jason Simon?" a lady in white asked.

"yes"

"well he is doing perfectly fine absolutely nothing wrong with him. He only passed out. But there were no scratches, scrapes, strained, fractured, or broken anythings."

"oh good" we all let out a sigh of relief.

We could finally go home. School was canceled the next day because the AC went out and it was way too hot without it. So it was a party, well a boring, quiet, small party, with me, Mitch, Ava, and Jason. Jason fell asleep while Ava just kind of laid there next to him pretty much asleep. And Mitch and I played just dance. What? Just dance at like 9 at night? All normal people do that! We played that for about an hour. Then we decided we were hungry. Macaroni it was. I stood in front of the stove stirring the macaroni, milk, butter, and cheese together. Then I felt Mitch's finger poke my sides. I screamed and turned just running into him again.

"Mitch!!!!!!! I've told you not to do that!!"

"oops!"

He poked my sides again. I started punching his chest. He wrapped his arms around me taking my hands behind my back so I couldn't punch him. I tried breaking free but I was against Mitch so it wasnt worth it but I still tried. He picked me up and threw me over his shoulder and held me there so there was no way I was getting down. He spun me around the kitchen.

"Mitch put me down!!!"

"never!"

"the macaroni though!"

"it's ok, I got it"

He left me on his shoulder with his left hand around my waist so I wouldn't fall. He finished making the macaroni, took it and me to the living room. He set the macaroni down but still had me as he got a movie.

"what movie did you get?"

"Aladdin"

"yay!!"

This is the best movie ever! We sat there with the pot of macaroni (dishes were to complicated), watching the movie. I curled up next to him and put his arm around me.

"so we leave Friday." he broke the silence between us.

"Friday?! No, why so soon! Why do you have to go too?"

"we are looking for a house it's ok. We aren't moving yet. We might not even be moving"

"but still I can't got a week without you! You have to call me every night and text me 24/7 and snapchat and face time so I can see your face and-"

"ok I'll call everyday. Text you every day. Sing you to sleep through face timing every night."

"you better!"

"I will!"

"and you have to come back!"

"do you think I wouldn't?"

"ya never know."

"It will be hard even to live a week without kissing your lips, or holding your hand, or being with you, or even being across the street."

"well you better not die on me and you can only be gone for a week tops!"

"I'll try not to."

"pinky promise?"

"pinky promise!"

Our right pinkies locked, our eyes met and our lips met our hands.

Chapter 13

Chapter 13

I woke up with my head on Mitch's strong chest. He didn't go home? Oh his parents are out of town. I started to get up off the couch but Mitchs arm was too strong around my waist. He was awake but kept his eyes closed. I could see him start to smile.

"Mitch let go!"

No response. I tried to get up again but his grip just tightened.

"Mitch I know you're awake!"

He let go and I rolled off the couch onto the floor. I went up stairs put on a plain gray t-shirt, capris, threw my hair up in a messy bun and put on a bandana. I ran down stairs to have a package of pop-tarts thrown in my face.

"race you to the river!"

"Regina not now! No regi!" I heard him yelling after me as I ran out the door.

I climbed up in my tree and Mitch in his. We both went to the area where the tree branches combined.

"remember the first day we kissed?" he asked.

"ya, what about it?"

"that was one of the happiest days of my life."

"why?"

"I don't know how to explain all I know is I love you and I never want to loose you. And if I ever broke your heart I don't think I could live with myself."

"you not being able to live with yourself would be what would break my heart."

The next two days were sad, because I knew it was time for Mitch to leave for a week. Then possibly forever. I stood there in his driveway before he and his family left for the airport. Starring into his eyes about to cry. I looked at the ground with my eyes starting to tear up. He hugged me and whispered:

"its only a week ok?"

Then he kissed me.

"I love you and I'll miss you Mitch"

"I love you too and miss you too beautiful"

He and his family got in the car and headed out. I stood in his driveway and blew him a kiss. He put his hand out to 'catch' it and pressed his hand on his lips as if to kiss it too. He waved goodbye and did the I love you with his hands then was out of sight for a week.

Chapter 14

I couldn't talk to Mitch while they were flying so for two days I sat by the river in my tree doing absolutely nothing. I would snapchat him, text him, leave him messages, so he would get them when he landed.

School on Monday thomas talked to me all day. We were becoming good friends. Which was good because I don't have that many. I told him about my dad and my mom. How my dad died when I was 9 in a terrible car accident. And my mom hating me. And how I was in love with Mitch.

Mitchs plane landed at 6:00 go I got to talk to him some. He wasn't able to face time me that night though. I was bored out of my mind. No Mitch to brighten my days.

My mom yelled at me for nonsensical things that I didn't do. I just zoned her out so I didn't really hear what she said.

I got a text from thom. 'check instagram'

'why?'

you're not going to like Mitch's picture!'

I went to instagram and started scrolling down to see a picture of a blonde curly haired blue eyed girl kissing Mitchs cheek. With hashtags of neighbors, cutie, and boyfriend.

Chapter 15

Chapter 15

M ITCHS P.O.V

"give me back my phone!"

"ok, here"

"Kathy! What have you done?!!"

"got you a girlfriend!"

"I have a girlfriend thank you very much!"

"me!"

"no! Not you!"

I shoved her out of the room and locked the door. Ugh!! Regina is going to think I cheated on her! I texted rae;

'I just met Kathy and she "fell in love with me" then she took my phone and did who knows what. After she kissed my cheek I slapped her. I don't like her at all. Nothing is going on between us, except for hope of never seeing her again.'

She texted me back.

'whatever! Then why is she where you are at if you just met her? And how did she get your phone? You said you were going to find a possible house. Not a new girlfriend!'

'I said she thought she 'fell in love with me'. I was getting it out to call you because I had time. I didn't realize she was behind me. I don't want a new house or new girlfriend. You don't realize how much I want to be with you right now!'

She texted back with more questions and more accusing.

REGINAS P.O.V.

I texted Thomas everything. What Mitch said happened and asked what to do. He texted back immediately;

'I don't care what you do. You're on your own. Tomorrow everyone will know of your problems with your mom and how daddy's princess is heartbroken by his death and her cheating boyfriend. Oh look it's already all over the Internet.'

What?! I thought I was able to trust Thomas. But all he wanted was to build me up so he could shred me apart. Because that's what was happening to me. I was falling apart and loosing myself to the words and lies of others.

...

After declining 437 face times from Mitch, I picked up on the next one.

He had a guitar in his hands and his face was gorgeous. He looked tired, like he had been crying some too, and his hair was a mess. Even if I wasn't sure to believe him or not, or to be mad at him or not, I still loved seeing him. I set my pillow up so all he could see was my eyes up.

He looked at me (well his phone but ya know) and sighed while his face became sad. He didn't say anything. He just started playing the guitar. I won't give up by Jason mraz. His voice was beautiful. I had to believe him. Mitch never lied. And I could tell he didn't do anything. He finished the song.

"please believe me."

I just nodded my head and he smiled.

"when will you be home?"

"saturday?"

"well tomorrows going to be hard without you, probably nobody will talk to me because of Thomas."

"what did he do?"

"told everyone about my dad and my mom and that you cheated on me even thought you didn't and who knows what else because I thought I could trust him."

"ugh I'm sorry regina. Just try not to get too caught up in it all. Okay?"

"okay."

"pinky promise?"

"Mitch this isn't going to work. It's through a screen."

"oh, ya. Then promise?"

"promise."

Chapter 16

Tuesday went as planned: terrible. Everyone knew everything. I went from being the girl who got picked on some to the girl who was liked and had friends and a boyfriend to the girl who had a "cheating boyfriend" and a terrible lonely life. It was worse than just being picked on. If I even tried to talk to someone that I was getting to know before they would say things like;

"Its no surprise your mom doesn't like you. Nobody else seems to either."

or "how's that love of your life treating you? Oh wait I guess he's just playing you."

or the worst one; "since you miss your dad so much why don't you just kill yourself and join him"

They don't realize what they are doing. Mitchell didn't cheat on me. And what if I did kill myself? They would be to blame. I wasn't going to kill myself. I never have and never will. But it does hurt, what their saying brings lots of pain. Why can't they just let me be? I've never done anything to them? Do they really wish me dead? What jerks if they do! Well there wish isn't going to come true. I may be hurt, but I'm not broken. Yet.

Mitchs voice was my lullaby to sleep. We were face timing again that night. I had a good long cry in front of him. I laid down on my bed and listened to Mitch singing 'safe and sound'. I was surprised he remembered I liked it. The last thing I remember was Mitch saying;

"their words are just words. But they are negative. If you let the negative in, the negative is what comes out. But let the positive in positive will come out and you will prove the world wrong.

Chapter 17

W ensday. Words. Worry. Wonders. Weeping. Waste.

Wounds.

Chapter 18

Chapter 18

M ITCHS P.O.V.

She Brushed her hair up behind her ear.

"regina, what's on your arm?"

She quickly put her arm down and had a shocked/scared look on her face.

"nothing it, it doesn't Matter."

"Regina."

"Mitch don't worry about it."

"Regina! why!"

"FINE MITCH. YA KNOW WHAT IM SICK OF ALL THE THINGS EVERYONE IS SAYING ABOUT ME! SURE SOME IS TRUE, BUT HOW THEY SAY IT MAKES IT WORSE. THEN THE OTHERS ARE ALL LIES AND JUST THINGS TEARING

ME DOWN. I CAN'T TAKE I ANY MORE! I FEEL LIKE GIV-
ING UP!"

She broke down in tears and hung up.

Regina don't give up. Not yet. There was nothing I could do. On the
other side of the country and no chance getting her to answer any
messages or anything. But I tried anyway.

She answered a face time in tears. She now had one of my sweatshirts.
And had the sleeves down to her fingers.

"Mitch look!"

She held up her phone to the computer screen so I could read it.

It was a text from Thomas.

'everyone would be better of you just killed yourself!'

"regina no!!"

"oh look! There's one from some random person I don't even know!
She said death is something you should really consider!" she said
yelling through her tears.

"Regina calm down! Breathe in slowly."

"Mitch I wish I could but I can't! It's just going to get worse tomorrow!"

"don't go to school tomorrow."

"well that won't be hard if I'm dead!"

She dumped a hand full of pills into her hand and threw the container at the wall.

"Regina! Don't even think about it! What good is it going to do? People are just going to get worse. If you kill yourself they win. They will not win." I slowed and quieted my voice. "Don't to it. Please Regina, don't."

She sat there blanked face and silent with the hand full of pills in front of her face.

"Regina."

No response. No movement.

"Regina."

Nothing

"REGINA!!"

She dropped her hand an the pills with it. She stood up looking terrible dizzy.

"ma-"

And passed out, bumping in to things while she fell.

"REGINA!!!!"

I quickly closed my laptop and call Jason.

"hello."

"Jason you need to go check on Rae. I just face timed her and she was about to take a hand full of pills when she passed out."

The phone was silent.

"I'm on it."

And with that he hung up.

"MOM!!!!"

"Mitchell! Quiet down your father is on the phone."

"mom we need to get home now! There's something wrong with Regina!"

"Mitchell, darling, we don't leave until tomorrow."

"not anymore. We leave now! My girlfriend, my best friend, Regina almost commit suicide!!"

"oh my! Go get whatever you need and let's go! James Mitchell and I are leaving to go home. There's something wrong with his girlfriend."

"what honey?"

"we are leaving to fly back to Florida, now."

"oh. Alright."

~~~~~~

We arrived at the airport in Florida around 6:40. By the time we left the airport it was 7:10.

"Mom can you drive any slower??"

"honey im going to speed limit, don't wanna get a ticket the first day back"

"my best friend could be dead and your worried about speed limits!"

I rushed into the hospital at 7:30. And ran up to the receptionists desk.

"where is regina Simon?"

"excuse me could I get you to fill out these papers before you go to see anyone."

"no! I don't have time for stupid papers! Where is Regina!?"

"are you a relative?"

"boyfriend/bestfriend/neighbor"

"does the family know you are here to see her?"

"I don't know!"

"well unless family says you can see her, you are not able to go in."

I just glared at her. I texted Jason.

'what room is she in?'

'256b'

"um excuse me miss. Where is the bathroom?"

"Down that hall fith door on the left."

"thank you."

I slowly walked down the hall and once I was out of sight I ran. I was stopped from opening the door when a nurse came out of her room.

"I'm sorry nobody is allowed to go in to miss Simons room at the moment."

"but u have to see her! Is-is she ok? What's wrong? How is she? I have to see her! Is she ok?"

"I'm afraid I can't answer any questions now."

"can't you open the blinds so I can at least see her through the window?"

"no they have to stay closed"

"Is her brother or mom here?"

"we sent her brother home a half hour ago. And her mom never came."

"can you at least tell me she is alive and is going to survive?"

"I'm sorry I'm not allowed to give any information related to her condition."

Chapter 19

Chapter 19

MITCHELL'S P.O.V.

"Shes sleeping but you may go in and see her now."

I got up from my spot in the waiting too and ran to Regina. She laid there so peacefully. I went over and sat next to her on the bed. I moved her head to my lap and played with her hair. I felt her shiver so I pulled the blanket on top of her. After a while I fell asleep too. I was awoken by Rae breathing deeply in her sleep. She had her head on my shoulder and hand on my chest. Her arm was covered in bandaged. I wrapped my arms around her fragile body.

"Mitch?" she didn't look up she stayed still. She was just unsure of who's arms she was in.

"ya?"

She smiled.

"you were really gonna do it weren't you?"

"......ya...."

"what made you not?"

"you. What you said. I don't remember what it was or what even happened that morning but all I know is I didn't because of you."

I leaned down and kissed her forehead.

"Mitch can you hand me that water?"

"sure sweets."

"thanks hots."

"I thought you didn't like that name."

"but that's when you call me it."

"oh ok hots."

I poked her side to tickle her. She jumped and laughed.

"Mitch!"

During her laughing she stopped and it seemed like she had trouble breathing. Then she coughed and turned her head as she got a strange look on her face.

"Regina you ok?"

"ya. Can you give me the water again?"

"here"

She swallowed and the look on her face made it look painful and disgusting.

"you sure you're ok?"

"I'm sure I'll be fine."

"ok. Oh I almost forgot. I brought you some roses, kit kats, and an Arizona sweet tea."

"aw Mitch! Thanks! Can you open the tea?"

"are you supposed to have it?"

"who knows. But I want it."

"ok..."

...

"hey pinky promise me something Rae?"

"What?"

"that you will be ok and be out of here soon."

"Mitch... I don't know if I can promise that."

Chapter 20

Almost Done

Hey so my story is ALMOST DONE!!!!!! only a few chapter left. anyway. I am sort of having a compitition for a story cover. so if you want to make one you can.

it needs to have story title : Pinky Promise,

and my username: eye_of_the_hurricane.

send it to my email: jasminarose51000@gmail.com

i will be deciding and changing it when i finish writing the story, so who knows when I will finish these last chapters but ya.

Chapter 20

M itchs P.O.V.

I stopped by reginas house before going to see her in the hospital. Shouldn't she be home now? She didn't even take all the pills.

"hello Mitchell! Is there anything I can do for you?" reginas mom asked.

"um I just wanted to get some things for regina. And are you going to see her today?"

"oh alright. And no I won't be going to see her at all. There is no reason for me. It was her choice to be there."

I didn't respond.

I went to her room and got the things I needed; her phone (which i dont know why she wanted, its filled with hate) her stuffed bear that I got her when we were like 8, and a sweatshirt. Oh look there is mine.

And without saying anything to her mom I left. I headed to the store to get another tea and a balloon. Out in the parking lot was, Thomas.

"hey how does it feel now that you're free?"

"um, excuse me?"

"you cheated on Regina and now you're single."

"I never cheated on Regina. And I actually have the privilege to call her my girlfriend. But you, you're part of the reason she is in the hospital right now."

"that's nice. Now if you don't mind I'd like to get a few things from then store."

"now if you don't mind. I'd like it if you would stop being such a jerk to Regina and everyone else."

We talked for a bit more then, let's just say I won in our little fight.

~~~

I stopped at her doorway to see Rae depressed looking, a tear on her cheek, starring off into space, and tubes running though her nose.

"Regina?"

"Mitch." she said crying a bit more.

"regina. What's with the, the- that?"

"ya know how my mom smokes? And the other day when I coughed and couldn't breathe right? You probably never noticed but that happens a lot. I try to hide it."

"but why?"

"I have lung cancer."

Who knew four words could destroy you.

"why do you just now have this then?"

"I never told anyone about the problems. They figured it out here. They say I've had it for a while."

"no no no no no no. No I can't loose you."

"Mitch it's ok. Lots of people have cancer. Ya but nobody that I know because they have all died from it."

Another tear rolled down her face.

"Regina I'm sorry. Is there anything I can do? And I brought your stuff."

"it's fine. No. Thank you."

"I got you another tea too."

"thanks. I can't have it right now though."

"ok."

I went and sat next to her on the hospital bed.

"Mitch why is your face bruised up?"

"um. I ran into Thomas."

"Mitch!"

"I didn't appreciate what he was saying so.... I won though!"

"nice."

~~~

After watching Aladdin for the seventh time that morning.

"so this isn't like anything very serious. Like you aren't going to die in a few minuets right?"

"they didn't tell me anything about that."

I could tell she was lying, her voice trailed off as she spoke. I didn't respond. I didn't know how to respond. So I just turned and kissed her. Holding her face in my hands. Her hands going through my hair. I could taste her salty tears that she had been crying all day. She had every right to be crying. She was dying and she knew she was too.

Chapter 22

Chapter 21

M ITCHS P.O.V.

Regina Simon died the next day. I never got to tell her I loved her one last time. Or tell her anything else I wanted to. And I never would. I kept the unopened tea can I gave to her, the dead roses, and I cry every time I go to the river with the willow trees. The happiness disappeared into loneliness. Her mom didn't cry over her death. She smiled inside the whole funeral. People at school didn't change. They didn't realize they added to her death. But they did. I lost my best friend, my girlfriend, my love. And nothing could undo it.

CPSIA information can be obtained
at www.ICGtesting.com
Printed in the USA
BVHW030844091122
651450BV00013B/747

9 781804 778913